On Post-Epic Or Imitative Words In Homer

Frederick Apthorp Paley

In the interest of creating a more extensive selection of rare historical book reprints, we have chosen to reproduce this title even though it may possibly have occasional imperfections such as missing and blurred pages, missing text, poor pictures, markings, dark backgrounds and other reproduction issues beyond our control. Because this work is culturally important, we have made it available as a part of our commitment to protecting, preserving and promoting the world's literature. Thank you for your understanding.

ON POST-EPIC OR IMITATIVE WORDS IN HOMER.

An examination of the language and vocabulary of the Homeric poems, archaic as they are in the main, tends to confirm very strongly the doubts I have expressed on other grounds, whether we do not commonly attach an extravagant and unreasonable antiquity to the Iliad and the Odyssey *in their present form*. I have shown good grounds for believing —indeed, I think it may be regarded as demonstrated—that a traditional epic literature of many dates and by many authors, orally transmitted and recited up to the time of Plato, was known to and received by Pindar and the Tragics under the general name of *Homer*. I have contended that the so-called "Cyclic" poems, distinguished in later times from our Homer by different titles and assigned to different authors, were, in all probability, but portions of the *Troica*, and of fully equal, if not of superior authority. The conclusion I arrived at was this; that our Iliad and Odyssey must be regarded, not as the original and older poems, of which the other Cyclics were but expansions and imitations, but as the *residue*, so to call it, or literary representative, of that great mass of epic poetry, reduced and adapted for transcription at some period not long preceding the age of Plato,[1] when the use of books (βιβλία)

---

[1] The very mention of ἀπόθετα ἔπη, 'rejected verses,' in Phaedr. p. 252 B, shows that in Plato's time the critical inquiry had commenced as to what

first comes into notice. They are largely made up of brief hints and allusions to the themes which the Tragics had at length; and though they embody some few episodes, as was natural, which Pindar and the Tragics had in the same or nearly the same form, still the general position appears to me unassailable, that *our Homer was not the Homer of the age of Pericles.* Still less, of course, was he the Homer of Solon and Peisistratus, as Mr. Grote and others so confidently maintain.

From this position, and from an entire conviction of its general truth, I do not recede, in spite of some real or apparent difficulties, and in spite of a good deal that has been urged, with more or less force, in numerous reviews of my former pamphlets on this subject.[1]

---

was and what was not composed by "Homer," who, it was felt, could not possibly have been the author of *all* that was then current about Troy and Thebes! We trace this criticism still earlier in the expressed opinions of Herodotus (i. 117, iv. 32), but the Tragics did not concern themselves with the question, nor did Thucydides, who quotes the Hymn to the Delian Apollo unsuspectingly as "Homer." In *his* Homer the Oaths of the Suitors and the raids in the Troad were recorded, as also the building of the fortified camp in the *first* year of the war.

[1] Some, as Prof. Mahaffy, accuse me of writing " arrant nonsense," and " betraying a slovenly way of thinking, and a want of grasping with clearness and firmness the general conditions of the problem" (Macmillan's Magazine, April, 1879). Others suppose I am defending an ingenious paradox, or have become so wedded to a theory as to force or distort every fact to suit it. I still fail to see any inconsistency in my main proposition, that Pindar and the Tragics followed an older ('pre-cyclic') and much fuller version of the so-called Homeric epics, either not knowing or not caring for the particular version which (whenever and by whomsoever first drawn up) does, *as a fact*, first appear as "the Homer" in Plato. If this proposition implies "confused thought," and a perverse manipulation of dates between Tragic and Platonic times, as Prof. Mahaffy says, I can only say, it is due to his way of putting my argument, and not to any inherent weakness in it, if rightly understood. When I speak of "the age of Plato," I mean, of course, the period during which his works were composed, or, roughly speaking, B.C. 400, and "the age of Pericles" B.C. 450. That Sophocles and Euripides lived till close upon 400, every schoolboy must know. If they had the same text or edition of Homer which appears to have been exclusively followed by Plato in his numerous citations, it is perfectly certain that they did not choose to follow it; and the probable reason is, that it had not yet become the popular Homer of the rhapsodists.

There is, of course, much in our Iliad and Odyssey which in matter at least, if not always in the form of expression, is very ancient. Such is the "Catalogue of Ships,"[1] evidently the work of some poet familiar with upper Hellas, and perhaps imported into the Iliad from the *Cypria*, or retained from another epic poem called (more appropriately than the present one is) by the same title of ' Iliad.' But the poems themselves have been so altered and remodelled by the rhapsodists of the later period that, however hard or impossible it may be always to separate the genuine from the imitative, or to assert that this particular verse is certainly very old and that comparatively new, they cannot fairly be accepted as evidence of anything more than of *the state of the epic dialect in the time of Plato*.[2] There are frequent allusions in them to the principal and most widely celebrated events connected with the history of the Trojan War, e.g. to the marriage of Thetis, to the rape of Helen, the embassy for her restoration, the building and capture of Troy, the wooden horse, the early adventures of Achilles, the return of the heroes, &c., which are mere incidents in our texts, but were histories, and long ones, in the time of the Tragics, and furnished the themes for

---

[1] There are vestiges of an ancient Κατάλογος Μυρμιδόνων in Π. 168 seqq. It is probable that many of the old epics commenced in this way, an example of which we have in the *Argonautica* of Apollonius. Compare Iliad B. 816 seqq., where we have a mutilated or abbreviated list of the Trojan forces. Both Herodotus and Thucydides follow these old precedents in naming the states engaged in the wars they describe, and so does Aeschylus in the *Persae*.

[2] A very large portion of our Homer seems to have been totally unknown to Pindar and the Tragic poets, and their *total* silence about many of the scenes which we most admire stands in marked contrast with others which are quite hackneyed topics in the tragedies. I have lately shown that ancient ballads on the Argonauts contributed largely to the composition of the Odyssey, and that the identity of characters in Apollonius Rhodius (Alcinöus, Arete, Scylla, Circe, Calypso, &c.) cannot have been due to their being borrowed from the Odyssey. This is an important evidence of the composite or derivative character of the latter poem as we have it. There are distinct and definite references to the Argonauts in H. 469, μ. 70.

very many of their plays.¹ This fact alone suggests the plain inference that something of the nature of an *epitome* of the Troica must have been made at some period long after the older and fuller epics had become popular; and that great changes were then made is indicated by the much more humane characters of Helen, Menelaus, Ulysses, in our Homer than we find in the tragedies. The great question is, when such an epitome was made. It seems extremely improbable that Pindar and the Tragics should knowingly and deliberately have followed the later more expanded and less authentic accounts. Such a theory seems the desperate expedient of those who are resolved to maintain the great antiquity of our Homeric texts at all hazards, and (as I think) against all evidence.

It is the object of the present paper to confirm the above view by a consideration of the *language* of Homer.² Those

---

[1] A volume might be written on the mere allusions in our Homer to the themes and narratives of the *Cypria* &c., such as to the Judgment of Paris, the rape of Helen, of Ganymede, of Thetis, the capture of Troy by Hercules, the fleet of Paris, the Greek ships at Aulis, &c. Such a verse as Υ. 147, ὄφρα τὸ κῆτος ὑπεκπροφυγὼν ἀλέαιτο is a mere hint as we have it in Homer; but the older epics gave it in full, from which Q. Smyrnaeus has preserved the account he gives in vi. 289, where he is describing the deeds of Hercules on Eurypylus' shield,

κεῖτο δ' ἐπὶ προχοῇσιν ἐυρρόου Ἑλλησπόντου
ἀργαλέον μέγα κῆτος ἀμειλίκτοισιν ὀιστοῖς
βλήμενον. Ἡσιόνης δὲ κακοὺς ἀπελύετο δεσμούς.

Similarly in Γ. 189 a single verse records the advent of the Amazons as Trojan allies, ἤματι τῷ ὅτε τ' ἦλθον Ἀμαζόνες ἀντιάνειραι. This was an important episode of the *Troica*, associated, in very ancient vase-paintings, with Hercules, but disarranged and disjointed in the *Cyclus*, in which it followed the Iliad, and now forms the subject of the First Book of Q. Smyrnaeus. Another instance is the slight reference to Memnon in Od. δ. 187, the theme of Q. S. Book ii., which describes an event familiar to Pindar and the Tragics. A third is the funeral of Achilles in Q. S. iii., briefly touched upon in Od. ω. Most significant too are the accounts in Pindar and in Quintus (iv. 145—170) of the deeds of Achilles, so widely differing from his adventures in the Iliad.

[2] Some years ago I printed, both in the Cambridge Philosophical Transactions and in the Journal of Philology (vol. vi.), some criticisms on the

who are familiar with Buttmann's *Lexilogus*, and with C. G. Cobet's hardly less important *Homerica*,[1] will be struck with the fact, that the probability of many spurious forms having been introduced into our text does not seem to have occurred to them; they had no misgivings of the general genuineness of "our Homer." Buttmann, for example, has eight pages to show that ὁ ἀγγελίης was an epic synonym of ἄγγελος " even in times of very remote antiquity," and as many on the question whether υἱὸς ἐῆος or ἐῆος meant 'your son,' 'his son,' or 'brave son,' from ἐύς. From my point of view I should argue, that a late rhapsodist who was familiar with ἀγγελίην ἐλθεῖν, 'to go on a message,' (like ἐξεσίην, 'on an embassy,') or with σοῦ ἕνεκ' ἀγγελίης, 'to bring news about you,'[2] mistook the meaning and invented such a phrase as ὃς Εὐρυσθῆος ἄνακτος ἀγγελίης οἴχνεσκε (O. 640). One who did not hesitate so to violate the digamma (Ϝάνακτος) would have little difficulty about ἀγγελίης = ἄγγελος. So υἱὸς ἑοῖο would easily be confused with υἱὸς ἐῆος, just as εὖτε (a word often so used in this sense by Quintus Smyrnaeus[3]) is mistaken for ἠύτε, 'as,' in Γ. 10, and T. 386.

I merely give these as examples, by way of illustration, of a possible or probable confusion. My present inquiry carries out the view which presented itself to G. Curtius, that our Homeric texts are a "vast patchwork," a mixture of very modern with very ancient forms of the language.[4]

---

apparent modernisms in the Homeric language. These points have been discussed by Dr. Hayman in his Preface to Vol. ii. of the Odyssey, and more recently by Mr. Lucas in the *Month* (July, 1879). A fair discussion is all that can possibly be desired, and I am glad to find that, although these writers differ from my conclusions, so much attention has been bestowed on what certainly is one of the most important questions affecting classical literature.

[1] Miscellanea Critica, pp. 225—430.
[2] Compare Soph. Aj. 221, οἵαν ἐδήλωσας ἀνέρος αἴθοπος ἀγγελίαν.
[3] E. g. in lib. i. 86, καί μιν προφρονέως τίεν ἔμπεδον εὖτε θύγατρα. So in iii. 142, 170, and elsewhere, but also in the usual sense of 'when,' as in lib. iv. 175.
[4] Greek Etymology, vol. ii. p. 207. Thus much (which indeed is all that

We accept the traditional Iliad and Odyssey as the genuine works of *Homer* on no valid evidence whatever.[1] All the real solid circumstantial evidence we possess (the writings of Pindar and the Tragics, and the still extant designs of the ancient vase-painters) seems entirely opposed to any such conclusion.[2] It is quite evident that *they* had a 'Tale of Troy' widely different from that which, in the main, though with some important differences from our texts, had become the *textus receptus* in the time of Plato. The loose criticisms and opinions of Herodotus, when carefully weighed, will prove, I venture to affirm, of no real literary value against the mass of evidence I have collected from the writers and artists of the Periclean age.[3] Now if the epic language or dialect was one which retained, as it did, a specific character for many centuries; if oral recitation, and not writing, was, as there is every reason to believe, the method by which the epic poems were handed down; if some forms and phrases, metrically convenient, or

---

I have contended for) is admitted by Cobet, Miscell. Crit. p. 402; where he maintains that "our Homer is a cento made up from the poems of many bards of different genius, ages, and countries." He differs from my view only in attributing a much earlier age to our existing texts, which he supposes, from their many Atticisms, to be the work of an Athenian Homer. But he must, to be consistent with himself, mean an Attic epitomist.

[1] There are good grounds for believing that the *Iliad* mentioned by Herodotus (ii. 116) was a different poem; for it contained an account of the wanderings of Paris, and it appears to be cited by him as distinct from the Διομήδεος ἀριστείη, from which he quotes verses (Z. 289—292) which do not now belong to the rhapsody so entitled, viz. Book v.

[2] The commonly-accepted theory, that these authors and artists knew our texts, but purposely avoided or deviated from them, I regard as very far-fetched and improbable. Indeed, I do not think it is worth serious discussion, resting as it does on a mere assumption, and a very unlikely one. It will satisfy no one who has thought on the subject at all.

[3] Neither Wolf in his *Prolegomena* nor Welcker on the *Epic Cycle* has gone at all into this question, or instituted any comparison of the tragic 'Homer' with our existing texts. Mr. Grote, who never touched this part of the argument, or went into any details about the language, (which indeed was not his special department,) though he suspected, with characteristic sagacity, the composite character of the Iliad, persuaded himself that, in its present form, it was considerably older than Peisistratus. But the evidence to *prove* this is totally wanting.

specially expressive, and bearing the stamp of antiquity on the face of them (e. g. εἰλίποδες ἕλικες βοῦς) remained unaltered to the last; was it not likely that along with these a large number of words of much later coinage (e. g. εὐαγγέλιον in ξ. 152) would creep into texts compiled for a literary purpose in a literary age?

Even in Pindar's time there must have been a kind of floating 'Tale of Troy,' since he speaks (Pyth. iii. 112) of 'loudly recited verses' (ἔπη κελαδεννὰ) being strung together by τέκτονες ἄνδρες, albeit the characters he specifies, Nestor and Sarpedon, have place in our Iliad. If these men had a written Iliad, the same as ours, in what sense could they be compared to builders or carpenters, and be said ἁρμόσαι ἔπη? It must refer to the custom prevalent in Pindar's time, of making connected narratives out of these stories, and putting them into different shapes and combinations according to the tastes or the requirements of the hearers.

On the theory of late compilation we *expect* to find mistakes as to the meaning of very ancient words, and great liberties taken in coining others on the same model; for the later rhapsodists may have been good poets and yet bad philologers. I hope to be able to show that such errors (if it is not presumptuous to call them so) are both numerous and grave. The marvel, to my mind, is that they have so long been accepted as genuine, and that modern criticism has made no serious onslaught upon them. The result of the inquiry, as it appears to me, is very damaging to the received opinions about the remote antiquity of our Homeric texts.

The mere fact, that the two poems are separate episodes arranged in twenty-four books in conformity with a general plot or plan, according to the *later* Greek alphabet, is enough to show a late recension. Still more significant is the structure of both poems on the assumption that all the events are already familiar to the reader. Thus, the Odyssey opens with allusions to the "Return of the Heroes," and even anticipates the story of the oxen of the sun and the Cyclops, α. 8, 69, β. 19, where the *name* of one of the crew killed and eaten is given, but not in the narrative itself, ι. 290. It could not do this, unless the adventures of Ulysses had been previously known in another form,—as indeed the appeal to the Muse, εἰπὲ καὶ ἡμῖν (α. 10) clearly intimates that they were. The arrangement of the Epic Cyclus, (of the date and authorship of which we unfortunately know nothing,) out of the vast materials regarded as Homeric by Pindar and the Tragics, undoubtedly tended to fix the still fluctuating poems in a more definite form. Before that time, it is quite evident that nearly or quite the same stories were told, with variations, of different characters. Thus, the prediction of the sea-god Proteus (δ. 475) is a variation of that delivered by Nereus to Paris (Hor. Carm. i. 15, 5), and Glaucus to Menelaus (Eur. Or. 364), while the transformations of Proteus are precisely the same as those attributed in the older tale to Thetis.[1] The games at the funeral of Patroclus were held, in another account preserved in Q. Smyrnaeus, over the body of Achilles. Both Achilles and Ajax were represented as ἄτρωτοι, invulnerable in fight. Ulysses dressed as a beggar in the presence of the Suitors is another version of his going as a spy into Troy, δυσχλαινίαις ἄμορφος, Eur. Hec. 240;[2] and similarly, as I have elsewhere said, Circe and Calypso are little more than *replicas* of the same character, that of the fascinating sorceress.[3] It is by this rearrangement of material that we can best account for the frequent allusions in our Homeric poems to the *Thebaica*. We find the explanation of this in the curious jumble of Homeric with non-Homeric matter in Q. Smyrnaeus, who was

---

[1] In Q. Smyrn. iii. 619, Thetis says of her reluctance to marry Peleus,
ἀλλ' ὁτὲ μὲν ζαὴς ἄνεμος πέλον, ἄλλοτε δ' ὕδωρ,
ἄλλοτε δ' οἰωνῷ ἐναλίγκιος ἢ πυρὸς ὁρμῇ.
In Od. δ. 456, Proteus, to escape being seized,
πρώτιστα λέων γένετ' ἠϋγένειος,
αὐτὰρ ἔπειτα δράκων καὶ πάρδαλις ἠδὲ μέγας σῦς,
γίγνετο δ' ὑγρὸν ὕδωρ καὶ δένδρεον ὑψιπέτηλον.

[2] Compare Od. δ. 244 with Q. Smyrn. v. 279.

[3] Compare especially ε. 61 with κ. 221; also ι. 29—32, where the two narratives are "jumbled" together.

evidently a late epitomist of the *Cyclus* as surviving in his time.[1] An Iliad existing in the time of Herodotus would necessarily become a very different one as a portion of the *Cyclus*, when a distinctive " Little Iliad " was first assigned to a different author.

In every theory which is incapable of absolute and direct proof, it is generally agreed, that if conditions are satisfied which the premiss leads us to expect, the hypothesis is established by a cumulative and presumptive proof of the highest kind that is attainable. In this way, and in no other, the rotation of the earth, the inclination of its axis, and the existence of a 'glacial period' have become accepted facts. No proofs to the contrary exist, just as there is a total absence of all proof that the Homeric poems in their present form have come down from a period four centuries earlier than Herodotus (ii. 53).

The more I study Homer (I am speaking, of course, only of my own impression), the more strongly am I struck with a marked *affectation* of antiquity. There is a mixture of archaic, pseudo-archaic, and comparatively recent forms, which seem to me in not a few instances to reflect the Greek of an age as late even as Theophrastus, or that which shortly preceded the (probable) age of the compilers of the Cyclus, and of the editors of Homer properly so called, i. e. the Alexandrine διορθωταί. It was impossible that they could distinguish verses six centuries old from those composed by clever imitators of the age of Plato. A large number of Homeric words, more or less peculiar in character, are common to Homer and the Alexandrine poets, and especially to Nicander of Colophon. It is a most important and curious question to decide (if it ever can be decided), whether they revived the

---

[1] In the so-called Cyclic poems attributed (in late times) to Lesches and Arctinus, there was a good deal of matter common to both, e. g. the contest for the arms of Achilles. K. O. Müller (Hist. Gr. Lit. ch. vi. § 3) accounts for this " interlacing " by supposing, what I suppose for " our Homer," that these poems were rearranged for the Epic Cycle.

use of such words, which had long lain dormant, from the ancient epic, or the words themselves are a recent accretion to and enlargement of the ancient epic, which, judging from the character of the words themselves, is my own opinion. As an illustration of this position, I would ask the reader if he believes ἀπογυιῶσαι, in the subjoined passage of Theophrastus,[1] was used with any intentional reference to Il. Z. 264,

μή μοι οἶνον ἄειρε μελίφρονα, πότνια μῆτηρ,
μή μ' ἀπογυιώσῃς, μένεος δ' ἀλκῆς τε λάθωμαι.

This is a fine passage, and one full of pathos; but I am not aware of any allusion to it in early poetry or art; and I observe that though the epic form ἄειρε is used,[2] it bears the sense which the word bore in the best Attic period,[3] πρόσφερε. This verb, ἀπογυιῶσαι, 'to unlimb,' or as we say, 'unnerve,' may well have been a wrestling term. Plato (Cratyl. p. 415) represents the perverse pronunciation of the rhapsodists of his day, μή μ' ἀπογυιώσῃς μένεος. They made μένεος depend on ἀπὸ, and thus other rhapsodists fancied that γυιῶσαι alone could mean 'to weaken,' and made up the verse in Θ. 402, γυιώσω μὲν σφῶιν ὑφ' ἅρματος ὠκέας ἵππους.[4] This is like what I must call the absurd phrase ὄχ' ἄριστος, a corruption from an old and genuine epic phrase ἔξοχ' ἄριστος, 'prominently and specially the bravest.'

Theophrastus uses ὑποβάλλειν, 'to interrupt,' and ζωρότερον πιεῖν, 'to drink stronger wine.'[5] Both words occur

---

[1] Char. xix. λαλιᾶς. Καὶ ὅταν γε τοὺς καθ' ἕνα ἀπογυιώσῃ, δεινὸς καὶ ἐπὶ τοὺς ἀθρόους καὶ συνεστηκότας πορευθῆναι καὶ φυγεῖν ποιῆσαι.

[2] Cobet justly suspects the form αἴροντας in P. 724 (Miscell. Crit. p. 401). But ἀρθείς occurs in ε. 393.

[3] Soph. Aj. 545. Ar. Pax 1, αἶρ' αἶρε μᾶζαν ὡς τάχιστα κανθάρῳ.

[4] Hesychius has γυιός· χωλὸς, νοσώδης, πηρώδης. This seems the invention of some late grammarian to explain a word which was used, contrary to all analogy, from an affectation of antiquity, i. e. it was introduced even later than ἀπογυιώσῃς.

[5] Char. xix and xiv. In T. 80, ὑββάλλειν seems to me an affected archaism. Late writers confounded ὑπολαβεῖν with ὑποβαλεῖν, in the sense 'to interpose.' Euripides has εὔζωρον μέθυ, Alc. 757, and the word

in the Iliad; but I am afraid that, like τὸ κρήγυον εἶπας in A. 106, and νέποδες in δ. 404, which are Alexandrine words,[1] their real antiquity is open to grave suspicion, especially as the digamma is omitted in εἶπας. It seems to me very improbable that such a verb as σιφλῶσαι (Ξ. 142) is of genuine antiquity, when σιφλὸς (our medical term *siphilis*) is known to us only from Apollonius, i. 204, τοὔνεκ' ἔην πόδε σιφλός. And though Aeschylus uses γνώμων, for one who has judgment about a person or thing, I very much doubt if ἤμονες ἄνδρες, *jaculatores* (Ψ. 886), is anything but a pseudo-archaic invention.

I further think, that such a vocabulary as ἀλλοῖος, γενναῖος, γνώριμος, πεμπταῖος, ὑγιὴς, ἀληθὴς 'honest' (Μ. 433), belongs rather to the dialect of the Pindaric or tragic, than to the ancient epic era. We have many Atticisms apparently even of a later school, e. g. ἐπίτηδες, 'on purpose,' σπουδῇ, 'scarcely,' ὁτὲ μὲν, 'sometimes,' answered by ἄλλοτε (as Plato has ὁτὲ μὲν—ἐνίοτε δὲ, in Phaed. p. 59 A), ἀμόθεν (α. 10), also Platonic, in the phrase ἀμόθεν πόθεν, εἰκὼς and εἶκε (Φ. 254, Σ. 520), οἱ ἀμφὶ Πρίαμον, 'Priam and his suite' (Γ. 146), the late Attic contractions εἶτε, ἐπιθεῖτε, the forms of the future κρεμῶ, ἐλῶ, δαμῶ, for κρεμάσω (turned into κρεμόω &c. for metrical convenience); so αἴρειν, ᾦξε, ἕστασαν, ἕστητε, ἑστᾶσι, ἀπετέθνασαν (μ. 393), κομιῶ, κτεριῶ, ἀεικιῶ, ἐπαγλαΐεῖσθαι.[2] To suppose that these forms of the

---

probably meant 'lively,' as Martial renders ζωρότερον by *vividius merum*. Yet ζωρὸς οἶνος would read strangely, I think, in Greek tragedy.

[1] Theocr. xx. 19, and xvii. 25, ἐοὶ νέποδες γεγαῶτες.

[2] Cobet (Misc. Crit. p. 309) admits that the Homeric forms γαμῶ, τελῶ, καλῶ, ἐλῶ, &c., "apud Athenienses tritissima sunt," and says (p. 307) "in omnibus his formis lingua Homerica ad amussim cum vetere Attica dialecto conspirnt." One would think that a large importation of Atticisms of the Periclean period was a much more reasonable theory than that such forms belonged to the language of B.C. 800. Cobet's convenient theory (p. 341) that Homer used either the resolved Ionic form or the contracted Attic form in such words as δήϊοι, ὑπερώϊον, ἠΐθεος, Τρωϊάδες, ἤϊα, seems framed to account for evident anomalies.

language existed two centuries before Peisistratus is to assume that the Greek language remained stationary for four centuries.[1] The general epic character of the Homeric poems is one thing; the class of words imported into it from the latest recensions is quite another. The argument, so often urged on the other side, that the whole style and conception, as well as the diction, of the Iliad and Odyssey, are manifestly very archaic, is perfectly worthless, and for this reason: *every* epic poem, however late, e. g. Apollonius Rhodius, Q. Smyrnaeus, Coluthus, has precisely the same general characteristics, and to the same extent. None of them, I believe, mention money, or law, or writing, or any existing political institutions of a later age. This depends on a fact which seems very little apprehended, that the Greek Epic had both *a style and treatment and a language of its own which never altered* (except by importation and accretion) *up to the latest times.*

"Everything in the two great Homeric poems" (says Mr. Grote[2]), "both in substance and in language, belongs to an age two or three centuries earlier than Peisistratus." He goes on to say that, as far as evidence internal and external enables us to judge, "we seem warranted in believing that the Iliad and Odyssey were recited substantially as they now stand in 776 B.C." These are most sweeping, and in my opinion, most unwarrantable assertions.[3] I contend that such evidence as

---

[1] I might add a rather long list of words which have a *characteristic* meaning in the dialect of Aristophanes and the Attic orators, such as περιδόσθαι 'to wager,' ἐνδείξασθαι 'to address a speech,' ποιεῖσθαι παῖδα 'to adopt,' παραβάλλεσθαι 'to endanger,' ἐπιδοῦναι 'to make a free present,' the rare and curious idiom μὴ πημαίνει, O. 41, as a formula of strong protestation, ἐπιβάλλεσθαί τινος in the sense of ἐπιθυμεῖν, &c. But I had rather call attention to the fact, and suggest inquiry how far this peculiarity of the Homeric language really holds good. I do not myself believe that such words as ὑπώπια, ἐπισκύνιον, φάεα 'eyes,' προσώπατα, πρότμησις, ἐπινεφρίδιος, and many other purely *medical* terms, are really very ancient.

[2] Hist. Gr. vol. ii. p. 161 (ed. 1869).

[3] In the same way of (what I call) random talk, Mr. Mahaffy speaks of "the irrefutable proofs that both the Iliad and Odyssey were not late compositions" &c. (Macmillan, p. 529).

there is (the testimony of the tragics and the details of ancient art, as well as that of language) is in favour of a very different conclusion. While such views pass unchallenged, and find a general reception (as they appear to do) on the authority of a great name, even among scholars, it seems to me impossible that any correct conceptions of early Greek literature should exist.[1] Mr. Gladstone, I need not say, has thrown his great literary influence into this side of the balance, and probably done more than any one else in confirming the *dictum* of Herodotus, that "Homer" lived 400 years earlier than himself.

It has very often been pressed as a fatal objection to the "late compilation" theory, that it is quite inconceivable that the old Homer should have quietly passed out of existence, and the new Homer succeeded to it, even in the historical period.

The objection itself shows how little thought has been bestowed on this question. The truth is, that so far from there being any *wonder* in such a result, it could hardly have been otherwise. The history of popular ballad-literature in all ages and countries (as distinct from writings reputed sacred) is doubtless the same. They tacitly follow the inevitable changes of age and language and popular taste, which likes novelty under the guise of antiquity:—

τὴν γὰρ ἀοιδὴν μᾶλλον ἐπικλείουσ' ἄνθρωποι,
ἥτις ἀκουόντεσσι νεωτάτη ἀμφιπέληται.

The existence of a vast mass of *Homerica* in the age of Pericles is no mere speculation; it is an ascertained fact, for not less than eighty known tragedies were composed from the *Troica*, and vase-paintings without end. That *somebody* drew

---

[1] Mr. Blaydes, in his note on Soph. Aj. 1031, says, "Homer represents Hector as already dead, when he was fastened to Achilles' chariot (X. 361 seqq.). Hermann and Wunder therefore think the text here corrupt, and that it should be altered to accord with the Homeric narrative." (!) There are allusions in that play to episodes more or less the same as we have in the Iliad; but the argument of the play is to be found in Quintus Smyrnaeus. See especially Aj. 1283 seqq.

up a Homer in a more compendious literary form, such as could be perpetuated in writing when, with greater facilities of transcription, a reading public came in, is another certain fact. It is a fact too, that such a cooking up and reproduction of the older epics *did* take place; for we find in Quintus Smyrnaeus, who lived three or four centuries after the Christian era, many minute details which appear with the closest exactness in the Greek tragedies, yet worked up in the style and the diction of the latest period. Why then may not the same process have been applied, some time during the age of Pericles, to the Iliad and Odyssey? What is the fact worth, that such an event does not happen to have been expressly recorded? It is only to *us*, who are interested in Homeric criticism, that the circumstance seems specially noteworthy. That our texts are made up from the Homerics used by the Tragics is proved by the constant allusion in brief to the older and fuller epics. But that any rhapsodist should have represented his version as in any sense *a new Homer* was plainly impossible. All the prestige and all the authority it could hope to attain depended on its being "Homer," and nothing but that. It was simply Homer no longer in detached episodes, but Homer in a readable continuous narrative, in such a form as, though essentially archaic, could be understood, and at such a length as did not exceed the still limited powers of transcription.[1] Before this, Homer was no fixed limited poem. Probably it was very much what any and every pro-

---

[1] I have elsewhere noticed the important and very interesting fact, that there is no vocabulary for any "pen-and-ink" process,—not even special terms for "reading and writing,"—earlier than the time of Plato. The writing on $\delta\acute{\epsilon}\lambda\tau o\iota$ and $\sigma a\nu\acute{\iota}\delta\epsilon s$ must have been far short of the multiplication of copies of literary works, even assuming, which, of course, I have no objection to concede (as I have no wish to be "relegated to Bedlam" by Mr. Mahaffy), that an author could laboriously write out his own composition. But I have a strong conviction that *a written Iliad and Odyssey was a comparatively late expedient*. Till about B.C. 400 there was no "reading public," and the infinite labour of writing such poems $\beta o v \sigma \tau \rho o \phi \eta \delta \grave{o} \nu$ would have been unrequited; in fact, Homer would have been thought "very slow" without the fire of professional recitation.

fessional rhapsode in every Greek city chose to make it. Only when it had assumed a written and a literary form it became *the* Homer; and then everything else became ἀπόθετα ἔπη and non-Homeric, the work of some *Scriptor Cyclicus*.[1]

I agree in the main with Prof. Kennedy (Studia Sophoclea, p. viii) that Thucydides "had no models before him but a few Ionic chronicles, culminating in the great work of Herodotus,"—though there is no proof that he had seen even that.

Dr. Hayman has endeavoured to prove (Journal of Philology, vol. viii. 15, p. 133—53) that a written literature was possessed by the early Greeks. To my mind, his reasoning is quite inconclusive. It is a very suspicious circumstance that none of the supposed early prose writers (Pherecydes, Acusilaus, Cadmus, Charon, Xanthus), are ever referred to by Herodotus or Thucydides; and though the former several times refers to Hecataeus, and the latter once quotes his contemporary Hellanicus, even this proves very little; for Hecataeus was a λογοποιὸς, and as λόγοι 'narratives' (Il. xv. 393) or 'anecdotes' or 'tales,' like the Αἰσωπικοὶ λόγοι were evidently composed for oral delivery by persons called λόγιοι, they may have been committed to writing long afterwards. Even Plato only once (Symp. 178 c) refers to a single one of these supposed "ancient writers," viz. Acusilaus. Add to this, the significant fact that the early philosophers Parmenides and Empedocles composed *in verse*. The teaching of all early philosophy was doubtless oral; so that the "writings" of Anaximander, Anaximenes, Heraclitus, &c., probably did not exist till the "literary age" of Plato. My doubt, if our Iliad and Odyssey were ever written out in the

---

[1] The names assigned in quite a late age to Cyclic or non-Homeric compositions are, in my opinion, of no real authority. This was a result of the compilation of the Cyclus, and the natural outcome of the suspicions and doubts which had long been entertained as to who and what "Homer" really was. Thucydides himself, as I have elsewhere observed, in his inquiries into the early history of Greece, i. 1—23, does not appeal to any written records, but to 'hearsay,' ἀκοὴ and μνήμη. Of the story of Alcmaeon he says τοιαῦτα λεγόμενα παρελάβομεν in ii. 102 fin.

Semitic fashion, from right to left, seems to afford Mr. Mahaffy some amusement (p. 528).

If the views of Dr. Hayman justify him in concluding that "at Solon's period or earlier, a Homeric text under the influence, unacknowledged at first, of written copies in aid of recitation had silently sprung up" (p. 144), I can only say, that my long inquiries into this question must have led me to a very erroneous conclusion. At present, so far as I can see, my learned friend and I must "agree to differ."

It is probable that the Tragics wrote their compositions on strips of wood, πίνακες, perhaps overlaid with wax, and deposited them, or at least such of them as had gained a prize, in the archives of the State. Something like these were the Θρῆσσαι σανίδες mentioned in Eur. Alcest. 967. From such tablets authentic copies of the plays were derived, directly or indirectly, some two and a half centuries later, for the use of the Alexandrian and other public libraries, from which they have descended to our times. They were composed, however, to be acted,—to be seen and heard, not to be read privately, as we now read Shakspeare.[1] Something would be learnt from a single verse in the *Supplices* of Aeschylus, in which βύβλοι are mentioned as a material for writing; but, unfortunately, there are grave reasons to suspect it is an interpolation. Of this, however, the reader may judge for himself, provided he has well considered *all* the verses in the tragedies in which the caesura is neglected. The passage is this (Suppl. 923):—

ταῦτ' οὐ πίναξίν ἐστιν ἐγγεγραμμένα
[οὐδ' ἐν πτυχαῖς βίβλων κατεσφραγισμένα],
σαφῆ δ' ἀκούεις ἐξ ἐλευθεροστόμου
γλώσσης.

Even were the second verse clearly genuine, which the metrical fault alone renders doubtful,[2] this mention of writing

---

[1] The contrary is not proved by Ar. Ran. 151, ἢ Μορσίμου τις ῥῆσιν ἐξεγράψατο.

[2] Dr. Hayman (Journal of Philology) says "the absence of caesura is a fact in favour of its genuineness. An interpolator would probably not have given a lame line." My study of tragedy leads me to a different conclusion.

'sealed down in folded pages of papyrus' as early as B.C. 470, could only refer to epistolary writing, and has no direct bearing on the copying of literary works.

What printing is to us, and what MSS. were in the middle ages, was in great measure supplied to the Greeks before Plato's time by paintings and sculptures. The enormous number of vases that have been preserved in ancient tombs up to our times attest this; and as many of them have written names, the word γράφειν, properly to draw or paint a design, came also to mean 'to write.' When Euripides says ὅσοι ἔχουσι γραφὰς τῶν παλαιτέρων, Hipp. 451, he undoubtedly refers to collections of painted devices illustrating mythological subjects, and not to written literature. Aeschylus uses the middle verbs γράφεσθαι and δελτοῦσθαι 'to write brief memoranda.'

The result of a full and impartial inquiry into the subject of ancient Greek writing is, in my opinion, this; that although the limited use of letters was early known and adopted for inscriptions and public records, a *written literature* was not possessed, nor even wanted, by the Greeks in the Periclean era. The long books of Hellanicus, Herodotus, and Thucydides could not have been *circulated* though they were put into writing by their respective authors at the close of that period.

In coming to any conclusion on this question, viz. the supposed extent of and the changes and variations in the old *Troica*, a much more extended study of the paintings on Greek vases of and prior to the age of Pericles is indispensably necessary. For this is almost the sole source of definite and accurate, because contemporary, information; and if it be found that their testimony is on the same side as Pindar and the Tragics, in the general non-recognizing of our Homeric texts, it is evident that the argument is immensely strengthened by the fact. Moreover, if the Homeric details of armour, chariots, walls and fortifications, are not earlier than those of B.C. 450, our notions of the great antiquity of these descriptions must be reasonably modified. I have myself carefully examined, with this object expressly in view, some thousands of Greek vases;[1] and nothing would interest me more than to find any subjects from the Iliad and the Odyssey depicted in any really archaic group.[2]

The comparison of Agamemnon (B. 479) with the broad-chested War-god is probably taken from some statue of the age of Phidias. The allusions to the Erechtheum (B. 549, η. 81), and to the offering of the peplus to Athena (Z. 271), and to the chambers of cut (or squared) stone, ξεστοῖο λίθοιο (Z. 244), point in the same direction, possibly the reference to the destruction of Mycenae, B.C. 468 (Δ. 53), and probably also the building of the towers and camp-walls with στῆλαι and other demolished materials (M. 258), which so closely resembles the construction of the old walls on the Athenian Acropolis.[3] These considerations, were it not for the very remote dated assigned to Homer, give weight to the opinion of Cobet, Misc. Crit. p. 281, "plurimis ex lingua Homerica indiciis colligimus Athenis oriundum fuisse poetam." Is not the obviously true account of the matter this,—that we have in our texts many passages composed by rhapsodes who were familiar with Athens in its most flourishing period,—just as

---

[1] The whole of those in the British Museum and the Louvre, with great numbers of others that have been engraved; yet these contain only a portion of these most precious monuments of antiquity.

[2] I think Dr. Hayman fails to establish any proof from this source that "our Homer" was the Homer of antiquity. But I hope the subject will be taken up with much more energy than it has hitherto been. Mr. Westropp, a high authority on Greek art, says "the Greeks who bore shields, helmets, and spears cannot in my opinion be earlier than the sixth century B.C."

[3] Mr. Tozer (Geography of Greece, p. 251) says that these walls still show on the north side "embedded drums of columns, the remains of the old Hecatompedon which was replaced by the Parthenon, thus confirming the statement of Thucydides as to the haste with which the city was fortified, and the use of the materials of public as well as private buildings in the construction of the walls." Compare Thuc. i. 93, οἱ γὰρ θεμέλιοι παντοίων λίθων ὑπόκεινται—πολλαί τε στῆλαι ἀπὸ σημάτων καὶ λίθοι εἰργασμένοι ἐγκατελέγησαν, with M. 258, κρόσσας μὲν πύργων ἔρυον καὶ ἔρειπον ἐπάλξεις, στήλας τε προβλῆτας ἐμόχλεον.

(21)

the *Catalogue* was the work of some one who knew Boeotia and its towns and villages?

From these introductory remarks, which in great measure are a repetition of what has been elsewhere said, I proceed to some critical inquiries into apparent anomalies in the Homeric language.

From a root καδ, a verb κάζω (for καδ-yo) was formed,—probably, like the cognate κοσμεῖν, a military term applied to the marshalling of troops. The passive perfect occurs in the best period of Greek literature, and we have φρουραῖς κέκασται in Eur. El. 616, εὖ κεκασμένον δόρυ in Aesch. Eum. 736, πανουργίαις μείζοσι κεκασμένον, Ar. Equit. 685, and so παντοίης ἀρετῆσι κεκασμένον in δ. 725, κακοῖσι δόλοισι κεκασμένε in Δ. 339. Here and elsewhere in Homer it is rightly used. But the late rhapsodists took it to mean not *virtute instructum*, but *virtute superantem*. Not finding a present κάζομαι in use, they referred the participle to a verb καίνυμαι, and thus we find such phrases as ἡλικίην ἐκέκαστο (B. 530), and Φρόντιν 'Ονητορίδην, ὃς ἐκαίνυτο φῦλ' ἀνθρώπων, γ. 282, τῇ δ' αὖτ' Εὐρύαλος ἀπεκαίνυτο πάντας ἀρίστους.

Curtius (Gr. Etymol. p. 138) says, " I have not made up my mind about the Greek καίνυμαι." In p. 228 he states the opinion of Legerlotz that δ has been changed to ι, as from a root ἀρδ, ῥαδ, come ῥαίνω and ἐρράδαται. But the meanings of κάζομαι and καίνυμαι are entirely different; they cannot be the same words.[1] It is conceivable that the latter meant the killing of an enemy in war, and so 'conquering' him. Compare ἄρνυμαι, ὄρνυμαι, τίνυμαι, αἴνυμαι, κίνυμαι, &c. When once the notion prevailed that ἐκέκαστο meant ' was superior to,' the rhapsodists gave it the construction of κρείσσων εἶναι,[2]

---

[1] Hesych. ἐκαίνυτο· ἐνίκα. Compare the Attic phrase ἀρετῇ σε νικῶ, Eur. Herc. F. 342. Thuc. iv. 19. This seems the prevailing use of ἐκέκαστο in the Iliad, perhaps from some fancied analogy with φαίνω, πεφασμένος.

[2] A similar affectation of antiquity, perhaps, is φθὰν δὲ μέγ' ἱππῆων, for πρότεροι ἦσαν, Λ. 51, and ὀψείοντες αὐτῆς, Ξ. 37, which is not, I think, from ὄψις, but from ὄψον, and the gloss of Hesychius may be thus emended: ὀψείοντες· ὀπτικῶς ἔχοντες, ἰδεῖν θέλοντες· ἢ βρωσείοντες, [ὡς] κλαυσείοντες.

and so we find in Ω. 546, τῶν σε, γέρον, πλούτῳ τε καὶ υἱάσι φασὶ κεκάσθαι.

Another very singular misconception is the use of χέρηα for χείρονα, and πλέες for πλείονες. An old word χέρης originally meant ὑποχείριος, or perhaps, 'a working man.'[1] It is rightly used in o. 324, οἷά τε τοῖς ἀγαθοῖσι παραδρώωσι χέρηες, in Λ. 80, κρείσσων γὰρ βασιλεὺς, ὅτε χώσεται ἀνδρὶ χέρηι, and Ξ. 382, ἐσθλὰ μὲν ἐσθλὸς ἔδυνε, χέρηα δὲ χείρονι δόσκεν.[2] But it is wrongly used in Δ. 400, ἀλλὰ τὸν υἱὸν γείνατο εἷο χέρηα μάχῃ, ἀγορῇ δέ τ' ἀμείνω, and in ξ. 176, καί μιν ἔφην ἔσσεσθαι ἐν ἀνδράσιν οὔ τι χέρηα πατρὸς ἑοῖο φίλοιο. It seems impossible, on any principles of language, that the accusative of χέρης should be the same as the accusative of χερίων (χείρων). This was a blunder of the rhapsodists who were no longer familiar with χέρης, and knew only of its comparative.[3] There are several words of this kind,—old terms denoting prowess,—which have mostly a corresponding superlative, but have lost the original form of the positive, e. g. βελτίων, ἀρείων, ἀμείνων, κυδίων, ὁπλότερος, φέρτερος, φέριστος, &c. It was not very unnatural to interpret such a phrase as χέρηα δὲ χείρονι δόσκεν by χείρονα ἔδωκε χείρονι.

Similarly there was an old adjective πλῆς, 'full,' which occurs in locuples, perhaps in plebs. In B. 129, τόσσον ἐγώ

---

[1] If this is the same word as herus (Curtius, Gr. Etym. p. 199), it must also have meant ὁ ὑποχείριον ἔχων.

[2] Similarly Quintus Smyrnaeus, i. 751, οὐκ ἀγαθὸν βασιλῆας ὑβριζέμεν ἀνδρὶ χέρηϊ. In vii. 71 he combines ἐσθλά τε καὶ τὰ χέρεια, by which he probably meant τὰ χείρονα. The various forms of the word indicate uncertainty as to the true use. In viii. 38 Quintus has Ἀχιλλέος οὔτι χερείω.

[3] The χέρηες were contrasted with the κοῦροι and κουρῆτες, the fighting class. (In Z. 59 κοῦρον is wrongly used in the sense of an infant.) It is an ingenious theory of Dr. Donaldson's that the legend of the Horatii and Curiatii came from the tradition of early conflicts between these two classes. The points of contact between the vocabulary of Magna Graecia and the Roman dependencies are numerous and interesting. Compare εἴρερος with servitus, νέποδες with nepotes, ἄφλαστον with aplustre, εὔληρα with lora (late Greek λῶρος), φέρτρον with feretrum, μήδεα φωτὸς with media (madya), ὑπ and ἀπ in composition with sub and ab, &c.

φημι πλέας ἔμμεναι υἶας Ἀχαιῶν, and Λ. 395, οἰωνοὶ δὲ περὶ πλέες ἠὲ γυναῖκες, it is clearly misused for πλείονες.

Between εἴσατο, an Ionic aorist from root ἰ, 'to go' (Curtius, Gr. Et. p. 403), having an affinity to ἀνέσαιμι, ἄνεσις, ξύνεσις &c., from ἀνίημι, and εἴσατο from root ϝισ, ϝιδ, there was a not unfrequent confusion. As ϝείσατο, ἐϝείσατο occur legitimately (in the forms ἐείσατο and ἐεισάμενος), the same metrically convenient inflexions were adopted for ἰέναι, which has no digamma.[1]

Another confusion is seen in ὄσσεσθαι and its compounds, which are sometimes referred to ὄσσε, 'eyes,' as in η. 31, μηδέ τιν' ἀνθρώπων προτιόσσεο μηδ' ἐρέεινε, i.e. μὴ πρόσβλεπε, sometimes (and correctly) to ϝόσσα, vox. In this sense it means 'to bode,' as in ξ. 219, οὔ ποτέ μοι θάνατον προτιόσσετο θυμὸς ἀγήνωρ. Hesych. προσδοκᾶν and προσδέχεσθαι. In X. 356, ἦ σ' εὖ γιγνώσκων προτιόσσομαι, it seems again to mean προσβλέπω (intueor, Doederlein). The digamma is violated in κάκ' ὀσσόμενος, A. 105, and κ. 374, κακὰ δ' ὄσσετο θυμός. Here again the rhapsodists were clearly at fault.

Another mistake is the confusion of ὄνασθαι, ὀνήσεσθαι, with ὀνόσασθαι. The former meant to get the benefit of some person or thing, to be 'blessed in it,' as we say; the latter meant 'to disparage,' 'blame,' 'be discontented with.' The Tragics often so use ὄναιο and ὀναίμην with a genitive, and in β. 33, ἐσθλός μοι δοκεῖ εἶναι, ὀνήμενος, the clear sense is 'bless him!' But it has no right to stand for ὀνόσασθαι, which is a totally different word. Yet in P. 25, we have

---

[1] Mr. Lucas, in a learned and thoughtful review of my *Homerica* in the *Month* (July, 1879, p. 367), suggests that καταϝείσατο (Λ. 358, 367, O. 544 Φ. 424) came from the fuller form of the root *ya* or *ja*, which appears in the transitive ἵημι, 'I make to go,' and in *jacio*. Thus he regards καταείσατο as representing καταjίσατο. Is not this virtually to make ἰέναι the same as ἱέναι? My explanation, on the theory of a confusion of forms by late rhapsodists, seems to me still the more probable view; and it is that maintained by Curtius, Gr. Et. vol. ii. p. 207. And if Mr. Lucas is right, how does he explain the absence of *j* in χροὸς εἴσατο, N. 191?

ὅτε μ' ὤνατο, which must mean 'when he spoke disparagingly of me,' and the attempt to explain it by ἀπέλαυσεν, ὄνησιν ἔσχεν (Hesych.), *cum me fruitus est* (Doederlein), is a failure. Moreover, in θ. 239, we have ὡς ἂν σὴν ἀρετὴν βροτὸς οὔ τις ὄνοιτο, and ὄνονται in φ. 427.[1]

The rhapsodists did not distinguish between ἑός, 'his,' σὸς, 'yours,' and ἠΰς, ἐΰς, (as in ἐὺς νόος, ἐὺς παῖς, Q. S. vii. 262, 365,) 'brave,' in the frequent combinations υἱὸς ἑοῖο and υἱὸς ἑῆος or ἑῆος. In Α. 393, ἀλλὰ σὺ, εἰ δύνασαί γε, περίσχεο παιδὸς ἑῆος, I do not myself doubt that the author of the verse meant παιδὸς σοῦ. Hesychius records the diversity of opinions in his gloss σεαυτοῦ and ἀγαθοῦ. Compare also Ο. 138, τῷ σ' αὖ νῦν κέλομαι μεθέμεν χόλον υἷος ἑῆος, and Ω. 550, οὐ γάρ τι πρήξεις ἀκαχήμενος υἷος ἑῆος, where the context strongly points to the meaning παιδὸς σοῦ, and in Σ. 138, πάλιν τρέπεθ' υἷος ἑῆος, to that of '*her* son.' In δ. 618, ἑὸς δόμος is *ejus domus*, and in ν. 320 φρεσὶν ᾗσιν stands for φρεσὶν ἐμαῖς.

This question however has been so fully discussed by Buttmann in the Lexilogus (who evidently was puzzled by the anomaly) that it is not necessary here to say more upon it. It was natural that ἠέος, by epic transposition ἑῆος, should first become ἑῆος and then ἑοῖο. The notion that ἑός meant both *suus* and *tuus* was suggested by the similarity of σὲ and ἕ. The later poets used ἑός very laxly, as Quintus Smyrnaeus ii. 28, μή νύ τι δειμαίνοντες ἑῆς χαζώμεθα πάτρης, for ἡμετέρης, and *ib*. 609, ὤλεό μοι, φίλε τέκνον, ἑῇ δ' ἄρα μητέρι πένθος ἀργαλέον περίθηκας, for σῇ.

A false analogy occurs in the occasional use of ἀτιμᾶν and ἀπατιμᾶν for ἀτιμάζειν or ἀτιμοῦν,[2] a false meaning in βοῶπις

---

[1] Curtius (Gr. Etym p. 715) distinguishes ὄνομαι, 'I revile,' from ὀνίνημι, 'I benefit,' and the two senses are remotely different. We have ὄνομαι, ὄνοσαι, ὀνοίμην, ὀνόσομαι, with an aorist ὀνόσασθαι, and ὀνίνημι with an aorist ὀνάμην, ὀναίμην, ὄνασθαι, future ὀνήσω and ὀνήσομαι, and a transitive aorist ὤνησα. The "epic aorist" is seen in ἀπόνητο and ὀνήμενος.

[2] Yet Sophocles has μὴ νῦν ἄτιμα θεοὺς, Aj. 1129. Cobet (Misc. Crit. p. 305) condemns ἀπατιμᾶν, but too hastily says "ἀτιμᾶν et ἀτιμάζειν passim leguntur."

for 'fair-faced,' or 'large-eyed,' as a complimentary epithet of women,[1] Γ. 144, Η. 10, Σ. 40, and false quantities in ῥῡσάμην, Ο. 29, λῦτο in Ω. 1, ἄτῐτος in Ξ. 484. Probably too ἐν καρὸς αἴσῃ was originally Κᾶρος ἐν αἴσῃ, 'no better than a Carian,' Ι. 378.[2] One may entertain doubts about Ποσίδηιον, ζ. 266,[3] ἀπείρηθεν (ᾰ) for ἠπείροθεν, (as if ἤπειρος was the same word as ἄπειρος,) and about the name Θρινακίη, which bears a most suspicious resemblance to the Magna-Graecia word for Sicily, Τρινακρία. It may be thought possible that in λῦτο and ἄτῐτος the dental was pronounced double; but no one can defend ῥῡσασθαι. The rhapsodists found ἐρύω and its short aorist, ἐρύσασθαι and εἰρύσατο, and they confounded it with ῥύομαι, ἐρρῡσάμην.[4]

The verb Ϝερύω, *traho*, is one of those which the later rhapsodists used sometimes with, sometimes without, the Ϝ. Thus we have νῆα μέλαιναν ἐρύσσομεν, Α. 141, τὸν νεκρὸν ἐρύσσομεν, Ρ. 713, but ἐπ' ἠπείροιο Ϝέρυσσαν in Α. 485. A comparison with *veru* seems to show that the Ϝ is part of the genuine word; but Cobet is mistaken in affirming (Misc. Crit. p. 266) "Verbum Ϝερύω, idem significans atque ἕλκω, habet *ubique*" (the Italics are his) "sine controversia digamma." See, for instance, Δ. 492, Τ. 311, α. 441, ι. 77. In this, as in many other words, as Ἴλιον, εἰπεῖν, ἴσος, ὅς (*suus*), ἰός *unus*, ἰδεῖν and its compounds, ἕκαστος, ἶφι, ἀνάσ-

---

[1] There can be little doubt now that βοῶπις, 'cow-faced,' was the descriptive epithet of the Moon-goddess, and attached to the Argive Hera, as γλαυκῶπις, 'owl-faced,' did to the Ionian Pallas Athene.

[2] Confused, perhaps, with ἐξ ὀρέων ἐπὶ κὰρ, and wrongly referred to κείρειν. Compare *capillus* and *caput*.

[3] I will just remark on the singular identity of the description here of an agora made of 'large stones sunk in the earth,' ῥυτοῖσιν λάεσσι κατωρυχέεσσι, with that recently discovered by Dr. Schliemann at Mycenae. That agora is mentioned by Euripides (Or. 919), but the broken pottery under it proved that it was not of a very early date.

[4] As in ἵημι, ἀΐσσω, ἰατρὸς, λύω, θύω, φύω, the long letter can be made short before the open vowel, so the naturally long ῡ in ῥύεσθαι is sometimes ῠ, as Aesch. Theb. 291, ξ. 107, and elsewhere. So we find δειλαῖος, γηραῖος, even πατρῷος. But, though φύω may be φῠω, ἔφῡσα cannot be ἔφῠσα, nor ῥῡσάμην become ῥῠσάμην, by any metrical licence.

σειν, ἔλπομαι, Ἶρις, there really is no consistency whatever in the Homeric use of the digamma; and one is again surprised at Cobet (Misc. Crit. p. 244) speaking of the "admirabilis linguae Homericae constantia."[1] In the matter of the Ϝ, it is quite impossible to reduce our texts to uniformity in this respect. Yet we now know, from numerous coins, vases, and other inscriptions, that the Ϝ remained in use till about B.C. 500, and probably considerably later. We can only say, that some Homeric words take Ϝ more regularly than others, e. g. ἔργον, οἶκος, ἄναξ, ἄστυ, οἶνος, ἡδύς, εἶδος, ἔπος. Yet all these are sometimes used without Ϝ. We find μῆνιν ἀποϜϜειπὼν in T. 35, but only a few lines further on (75) μῆνιν ἀπειπόντος. We have τὸ κρήγυον εἶπας, Α. 106, θύγατερ Διὸς εἰπέ, α. 10. If the Latin *vis, video, vestis, vicus*, prove anything, they show that εὖ Ϝειδότες ἶφι μάχεσθαι, Β. 720, ἐς δ' ἰδέτην, β. 152, λάϊνον ἕσσο χιτῶνα in Γ. 57, and ἀπήνυσαν οἴκαδε in η. 326, are not very ancient, while εἵματα Ϝεσσάμενος in β. 3 follows the old form. We have οὐδὲ μὲν ἔργον, Ι. 374, ἠδὲ καὶ ἔργον, Λ. 703, περὶ μὲν Ϝεῖδος περὶ δ' ἔργα τέτυκτο, P. 279, but ἀγασσάμεθ' εἶδος ἰδόντες, Γ. 224. Similarly in B. 750, οἳ περὶ Δωδώνην δυσχείμερον οἰκί' ἔθεντο might have been δυσχείμερα Ϝοικί' ἔθεντο, but the very next verse, οἵ τ' ἀμφ' ἱμερτὸν Τιταρήσιον ἔργ' ἐνέμοντο, cannot be so corrected. There are many verses in which the Ϝ in οἶκος (*vicus*) is violated, e. g. in Α. 19, ν. 121 and 125, π. 70. In Ω. 449 we find ποίησαν ἄνακτι, in ξ. 438 θυμὸν ἄνακτος. In Σ. 274, νύκτα μὲν εἰν ἀγορῇ σθένος ἕξομεν, ἄστυ δὲ πύργοι &c., in Ω. 320, δεξιὸς ἀΐξας ὑπὲρ ἄστεος, in γ. 260, κείμενον ἐν πεδίῳ ἑκὰς ἄστεος. So also οἱ and ἑ are used in place of Ϝοι and Ϝε, Ζ. 289, Τ. 282, Ω. 53, 72, Ξ. 162, ζ. 280. Yet

---

[1] I have elsewhere shown, that the Ϝ was retained, when metrically convenient, even by the post-Christian epic writers. The common argument, that Ϝ had begun to be a "fluctuating letter" as early as B.C. 850, the supposed date of the composition of the Iliad, shows very small knowledge of the subject. We often find in Q. Smyrnaeus Ϝίδον, Ϝέργον, ἐϜείδετο, Ϝάστυ, ἐϜαγὼς, ἐϜόλπει, and similar forms, though in most cases he takes pains to avoid the apparent *hiatus* caused by the lost Ϝ.

"non magis οἱ pro Ϝοι in lingua Homerica poni potest quam Latine *ibi* pro *sibi*" (Cobet, § 58). Similarly, we find δέπας ἡδέος οἴνου in γ. 51, μελιηδέος οἴνου ib. 46, Ω. 545, ὅθ' ἡδέι λέξεται ὕπνῳ in Δ. 131.

Cobet remarks (Homerica, § 39), "Ϝιδον Homericum est, non ἴδον." What then shall we say of the following passages? Granting that in Δ. 232 and 240, we might read σπεύδοντα Ϝίδοι for σπεύδοντας &c., we cannot get rid of εἴ τις ἴδοιτο and εἴ τιν' ἴδοιτο in Γ. 453, M. 333, nor of ἀχρεῖον ἰδών in B. 269. Similarly the Ϝ is wanting in ἐκκατιδών Δ. 508, H. 21, in ἦμαρ ἰδέσθαι γ. 233, ε. 220, in κακὰ πόλλ' ἐπιδόντα ('having *lived to see*') X. 61, θᾶσσον ἰδώμεθα λ. 44, σπέος εἴδομεν ι. 182 (Ϝίδομεν σπέος, Cobet), ἕλε πάντας ἰδόντας γ. 372, ἵν' εἰδῇς β. 111, ἐς δ' ἰδέτην β. 152, αὐτίκ' ἰδόντ' ρ. 327, μήτις ἴδηται φ. 228, ὡς ἐσιδέσθην ω. 101. I do not scruple to affirm, that the collective argument from the frequent violations of the true use of the digamma in our Homeric texts *conclusively* proves that they were largely made up in language and versification by rhapsodists of a comparatively late age.

For all these, and very many more, instances of vague and uncertain usage are precisely what we should look for on the theory of late compilation.[1] It is *possible*, no doubt, that in the genuine epic of antiquity such anomalies existed; but it is *infinitely* more probable they are due to the patchwork of much later ages.

Cobet has endeavoured (Homerica, §§ viii. ix.) to reduce all the passages containing inflexions from the root Ϝελ, (ἕλσαι, ἀλεὶς, ἑλίσσειν,) to uniformity in this respect.[2] Thus, in N.

---

[1] I never said, or spoke of, late *authorship*, which some, who have not looked into the question, supposed me to mean. I am contending against those who assume a written Homer from the time of Peisistratus. There is truth in a remark in the *Athenaeum*, that "*two* persons are required to tell a truth; one to speak it, and another to understand it" (July 26, 1879).

[2] He affirms that neither εἴλειν nor εἰλεῖν was the epic form, but that Ϝέλσαι came from Ϝέλλω as κέλσαι from κέλλω (p. 272). A comparison of

204, he would read σφαιρηδὸν δέ μιν ἧκε Fελιξάμενος, for ἧκε δέ μιν σφαιρηδὸν ἐλιξάμενος, and in several others he proposes ἐFέλιξεν, Fελιξάμενος for ἐλέλιξεν, ἐλελιξάμενος, &c. He suggests a few corrections where ἀνάσσειν, ὃς suus, and ἔλπομαι have no F. But my long lists of violated F in the Iliad and the Odyssey show that these attempts do not go far in removing this *vitium inveteratum* of the Homeric poems. In § xv. he contends that as οἶδα and ᾔδεα take the F, we should read ὄφρα Fίδῃ for ὄφρ' εἰδῇ in Θ. 406 and elsewhere. But he takes no notice of the many passages where such correction is impossible, as in κακὸς εἴδεται, Ξ. 472, κακὰ πόλλ' ἐπιδόντα, Χ. 61, θεοὺς ἐπιδώμεθα, ib. 254,[1] τό γε κέρδιον εἴσατο, τ. 283, ὑποκρίνονται ἵν' εἰδῇς, β. 111. In truth, it is very doubtful if ἰδεῖν was ever used as a synonym of εἰδέναι, and for this very reason ἰδέω χάριν, 'I shall feel gratitude,' in Ξ. 235, seems to me a pseudo-archaism. And this raises the question if the oft-recurring ἰδυίῃ and ἰδυίῃσι should not rather be εἰδυίῃ (which the metre will always admit), according to the Attic use, and not Fιδυίῃ, as Cobet and others assume. Such a perfect participle as ἰδώς is contrary to analogy, as ἰκώς for εἰκώς would be.

In § xlvii. Cobet notices the difficulty in the frequent use of the epic aorist δέγμενος and ποτιδέγμενος in the sense of προσδοκῶν, 'waiting for,' as in I. 191, δέγμενος Αἰακίδην ὁπότε λήξειεν ἀείδων. He thinks that δέχμενος, a form preserved by Hesychius, should in all cases be restored; and he contends that δεδεγμένος in Θ. 296, Ψ. 273, and δεδοκημένος in O. 730 are used by the poet (like οἶδα) in a present sense. In defence of δέχμενος he cites ἄρχμενος, found in more than one fragment of Callimachus for ἀρχόμενος.

---

volvo would show that FέλFω, not Fέλλω, was the original word. Compare ὕλFη with *silva*. Even these two words, in my belief, belong to the same root as *pilus* and our *felt*, and denote the dense crowding or packing of trees. A trace of the second F remains in εἰλύω, εἰλυμένος. Compare λύω with *solvo*, *silüa* and *silva*.

[1] A very obscure expression. Perhaps ἐπιδόσθαι was meant, 'let us mutually offer the gods as witnesses.'

We might just as well expect τίθμενος for τιθέμενος.¹ As for ὅρμενος, which he says is for ὀρόμενος, it is clearly an epic aorist, and ἐδέγμην in ι. 513 is analogous to ἐλέγμην ibid. 335. Either this δέχμενος was a figment of late rhapsodists, or, like the participle ἰών, the aorist was used both in a past and a present sense. Cobet therefore may be right in replacing δέχμενος, but wrong in supposing it a genuine archaic form.²

The same criticism, I think, viz. an affectation of antiquity, applies to A. 291, τοὔνεκά οἱ προθέουσιν ὀνείδεα μυθήσασθαι; 'Do they therefore put before him reproaches to utter against others?' Here Bekker reads προθέωσιν in the sense of προθήσουσιν, and Doederlein refers the compound to θέω, *curro, ideone ei procurrunt verba dictu contumeliosa?* which, if not downright nonsense, is closely allied to it. The poet can only have meant προτιθεῖσι, as αἰτίαν προθεὶς is used in Soph. Aj. 1051. Similarly in λ. 584, it is said of Tantalus standing in the lake, στεῦτο δὲ διψάων, which, as the context shows, must mean *stabat sitiens*. But this is a false use of the word, which always means *statuit* in the sense of moral determination, e. g. in B. 597, στεῦτο γὰρ εὐχόμενος νικησέμεν, and Φ. 455.³ Some rhapsodist in the post-epic times introduced forms which he thought justified by the futures θήσω and στήσω.

Such a verb as πινύσσειν, 'to be prudent,' πινυτὸν εἶναι, is conceivable on the analogy of πλανύττειν, ὀνειρώττειν, ὑγρώσσειν, and ὑπνώσσειν (the last two Aeschylean words).

---

¹ It may be suggested that the plural forms δέχατο, ἔρχατο, ἐπώχατο (M. 340) may be thus explained, viz. by the omission of the connecting letter, for δέχ-ντο &c. Perhaps too such forms as ἔοιγμεν and ἐπίπιθμεν (B. 341) follow the same principle. Still, I think this δέχμενος is destitute of any real ancient authority.

² In the later epic (Quintus Smyrnaeus iii. 755) a form δέχνυσθαι was introduced.

³ Hesychius, στεῦτο· κατὰ διάνοιαν ἵστατο καὶ διωρίζετο, ἢ διεβεβαιοῦτο, i. e. *animo statuebat et decernebat*. Curtius, Gr. Etym. p. 216, strangely mistranslates this "he stands or is fixed in a certain direction."

But the transitive use, 'to instruct,' in Ξ. 249, ἤδη γάρ με καὶ ἄλλο τεῇ ἐπίνυσσεν ἐφετμῇ, is contrary to analogy;[1] the active verb is πινύσκειν, like διδάσκειν, μεθύσκειν. So in Aesch. Pers. 825,

πρὸς ταῦτ' ἐκεῖνον, σωφρονεῖν κεχρημένον,
πινύσκετ' εὐλόγοισι νουθετήμασι.

As for ἀπινύσσειν = ἄφρονα εἶναι (O. 10), like ἀηθέσσειν and ἀγνώσσειν, (ἀγνώσασκε in ψ. 95 is a form altogether unintelligible, unless from the barbarism ἀγνώω,) I cannot help thinking they are the coinages of the Alexandrian mint, and perhaps the same is true of καπύσσειν, X. 22.

Nor is it possible, I conceive, to defend τετευχώς, *factus*, μ. 423, τετευχῆσθαι, *armatum esse*, χ. 104, γέφυραι ἐεργμέναι, 'artificial dams' (as if from ἔργω, for εἴργω here gives no sense). Such short forms as βλάβει and τέμει seem as much against analogy as τύπω for τύπτω would be.[2] So ἀφύω, ὑφᾶν, ἀφᾶν, ὑλᾶν, σκεπᾶν (ν. 99), for ἀφύσσω, ὑφαίνω, ἅπτεσθαι, ὑλακτεῖν, σκεπάζειν, such aorists as ἤσατο, χήρατο, ἐπεμήνατο, perfect participles like ἠσχυμμένος (Σ. 180),[3] μεμορυχμένος, βεβροτωμένος, ῥερυπωμένος, κεκακωμένος, ἐκπεπαταγμένος,—all these seem to be open to the suspicion at least of belonging to a comparatively late age.

A strange use is δαίμονα δοῦναι, Θ. 166, and πρὸς δαίμονα, *contra fatum*, P. 98, 104. Euripides has a phrase not unlike it, Phoen. 1653, οὐκοῦν ἔδωκε τῇ τύχῃ τὸν δαίμονα, but the reading is open to suspicion. So δαίμονος αἶσα in Q. Smyrn.

---

[1] ἰχθῦς ἀγρώσσων in ε. 53 is but a synonym of ἀγρεύων, and ἀγρεύειν = ἀγρεὺς εἶναι, and takes an accusative, like many other neuter verbs in —εύω, from the sense implied.

[2] I believe such words were late inventions from false or genuine aorists, such as ἔβλαβεν, Q. Smyrn. v. 509, ἔκρυφε ib. vii. 235. Thus ἰδήσω was formed from ἰδεῖν, ἐνισπήσω from ἐνισπεῖν, χραισμήσω from χραισμεῖν, δεδοίκω and πεφύκω from δέδοικα and πέφυκα.

[3] Compare a scholiasts' word (on Ajax 334) παρωξυμμένος. The Tragics use ἐρριμμένος, τετυμμένος, κεκρυμμένος, but these have no real resemblance to ἠσχυμμένος, which is something quite τερατῶδες. Herodotus and Thucydides use κεκακωμένος.

i. 104, iii. 374, &c., savours of the post-epic vocabulary. In Od. λ. 61 we are sure the verse is not very ancient, ἆσέ με δαίμονος αἶσα κακὴ καὶ ἀθέσφατος οἶνος (Ϝοῖνος). Here there is an intentional play on ἆσέ με αἶσα, and the absence of the Ϝ in οἶνος is a proof of late composition. It should be observed, that δαίμων in Homer is used both for θεὸς and τύχη, but nowhere in the Aeschylean sense of a departed spirit with power over the living.

The curious word ὤρεσσι, *uxoribus*, and the hardly less strange form ἄωροι, 'dangling,' applied to the feet of the monster Scylla, in μ. 89, deserve attention, as perhaps words of the later epic period.

Cobet somewhere remarks that ἀείρειν bore a meaning analogous to ἅμα and εἴρειν, *conserere*, 'to string together.' The root of εἴρειν is σϜερ or *svar*, so that ἀϜείρειν is the same as the Attic αἴρειν. There are four meanings attached to this word, (1) to lift or hoist; (2) to bring; (3) to tie together; (4) in the middle, to win or carry off, as κῦδος ἀρέσθαι &c. Perhaps the notion of lifting by means of a rope, like a stone hoisted by a pulley, was the primary one. But the idea of tying together prevails in συνάορος, a wife, ξυνωρὶς, yoked horses, and παρήορος, a trace-horse. Very probably ἀὴρ, which took the Ϝ, αὐὴρ, is, like the Saxon *lyft*, 'the raised sky,' and not from ἄω, *spiro* (Curtius, p. 390). There were three nouns, ἄορ a sword, ἄορ a caldron (ρ. 222), and ἄορ a wife. This last took the contracted form ὤρ, and ἄορες became ὦρες, as τιμάορος became τιμωρὸς, and hence in the dative the Homeric ὤρεσσι.[1]

But ἄορ in the last sense became (perhaps for distinction) ὄαρ (ὄϜαρ), and from this was formed ὀάρων, *uxorum*, I. 327,[2]

---

[1] The original Ϝ would seem to have been retained, as we have ἀμυνέμεναι Ϝώρεσσι. Cobet (Misc. Crit. p. 405) blames Bekker without reason for the form Ϝοάρων (i. 327).

[2] Hesych. recognises both ὄαρες and ὄαροι in the sense of γυναῖκες, and he rightly adds ἀπὸ τοῦ συνηρμόσθαι. The Latin *conjux* and *uxor*, both from the root *jug*, are exact synonyms.

ὀαρίζειν and ὀαρισμὸς, in the sense of conversing, usually, though not always, in the language of lovers. By the interchange of long with short syllables, μετήορος became μετέωρος, ἤορος ἄωρος, and ἀπήορος, 'hanging far off,' ἀπήωρος, a term applied to the roots of a fig-tree in μ. 435.

I have elsewhere remarked[1] that there were many words of double or ambiguous use, between the meanings of which the later rhapsodists were perplexed. This subject is very curious, and I here mention some of these, the discussion of context and etymology being too long for the present work; ἰσχανᾶν 'to hold back' (E. 89) and 'to eagerly desire'[2] (P. 572), τραπῆναι 'to turn' confounded with ταρπῆναι 'to enjoy' (Γ. 441, Ξ. 314, θ. 292, compared with ε. 227), ἄλλεσθαι with πάλλεσθαι, σκέπτεσθαι from σκεπ 'cover' and σκοπ 'see'; ὄσσεσθαι from ὄσσε oculi and Fόσσα vox; ἀνέσαι from ἀνίημι and root ἐδ, ἐδανὸς from ἀδ (σFαδ) and ἐδ, ἐεργμένος from Fεργ facere and claudere (E. 89), ἔλσας from Fελλειν and ἐλαύνειν (ε. 132, 367, ν. 164), εἴσασθαι from Fιδ and the aorist of ἰέναι, ζωγρεῖν from ἀγρεύειν and ἀγείρειν (E. 598), &c.

Not less worthy of inquiry are the endless *repetitions* of verses and passages in both poems. These are so numerous, often with slight variations, that they form in themselves the strongest possible argument for the theory of late rhapsodists drawing from a common stock of matter. I am quite sure that no poet, however voluminous, ever repeated many hundreds of his own verses! But this is precisely what must *of necessity* have taken place in the late compilation and arrangement of epics separately recited by many composers.

The foregoing remarks will be uninteresting to the many, but perhaps they may engage the attention of the few. The extravagant antiquity of the poems that have come down to us

---

[1] Journal of Philology, vol. vi. p. 185.
[2] Compare ἴχαρ, γλίχεσθαι. The rhapsodists mistook the original word, pronounced ἰκχανδα &c.

really rests on no evidence whatever but that of tradition, which, properly speaking, is not evidence at all. Slight as it is in itself, it is entirely neutralized by the fact, about which there can be no doubt, that any and every epic about Troy or Thebes in ancient times was attributed to "Homer." It is easy to opine with Cobet (Homerica, § 12) that "in the old Ionic ballads which bear the name of Homer, there were many MS. corruptions (mendose scripta) and interpolations *jam ante Solonis aetatem;*" but it is an opinion that is the merest conjecture. I do not believe in MSS. of Homer of anything like such an age as this. I should, of course, be very glad to believe that the Iliad and the Odyssey justly claim the great antiquity ascribed to them; but at present I hold that, though tradition is in favour of such a view, evidences both internal and external are very strongly against it.

To my mind, there have been two fallacies generally prevalent, 1. that Homer was very early committed to writing, and 2. that the Iliad and the Odyssey were the original poems, of which the other "Cyclics" were mere supplements. I believe they contained matter older and more genuine than our poems in their present form, which in fact are based on earlier materials, with large modifications and additions; and that this is the simple reason why Pindar and the Tragics and the vase-painters show little or no acquaintance with the texts that have come down to us.

From my point of view, of course, I contend that the Homeric language is to a great extent *imitative*, and includes many forms introduced on fancied analogies and resemblances, but not the result of a healthy and spontaneous growth. I seem to myself to have raised a question of tremendous interest; and these few pages contain the thoughts of many long years. I never felt the least wish to dogmatize in such a matter, but only to invite fair and courteous discussion. It is hardly surprising that my view has been met with incredulity and apparent prejudice, where it has been dealt with by reviewers, many of whom too clearly show that they have never understood the real difficulties of the position they defend. It was a wise remark of an old scholiast,[1] πάντες ἄνθρωποι πρὸς τὸ ἀληθὲς ἀγανακτοῦσι καὶ ἀντιλέγουσιν. It may be that few like to have their convictions on literary matters disturbed, and it may seem to them but an ungracious task to disturb them. Such persons must console themselves with the good old saw, ὀρθὸν ἀλήθει' ἀεί.

---

[1] On Soph. Ajax 1328.

INDEX.

A.

ἀγγελίης (ὁ) 7
ἀγνώσασκε 30
Acusilaus 17
ἀείρειν, αἴρειν, 12. 31
ἀηθέσσειν 30
ἀήρ 31
Αἰσωπικοὶ λόγοι 17
ἀκοή 17 note
Ἀμαζόνες 6 note
ἀμείνων 22
ἀνάσσειν, ἄναξ, without F, 7. 25—6. 28
ἀνέσαι 23. 32
ἄορ 31
ἀπατιμᾶν 24 note
ἀπειπεῖν, ἀποϜειπεῖν, 26
ἀπείρηθεν, ἠπείροθεν, 25
ἀπήωρος 32
ἀπινύσσειν 30
ἀπογυιῶσαι 12
ἀπόθετα ἔπη 1. 17
ἀρείων 22
ἁρμόσαι ἔπη 9
ἄρχμενος 28
ἆσέ με αἶσα 31
ἄστυ, Ϝάστυ, 26
ἀτιμᾶν, ἀτιμοῦν, 24 note
ἀτῖτος 25
Atticisms in Homer 13—14
αὐὴρ, ἀϜὴρ, 31
ἄφλαστον, aplustre, 22 note
ἄωρος 31—2

B.

βεβροτωμένος 30
βελτίων 22
βιβλία, libri, 1
βίβλοι, βύβλοι, 18
βλάβω 30
βοῶπις 25

Γ.

γέφυραι ἐεργμέναι 30
γλαυκῶπις 25 note
γλίχεσθαι, ἰχάρ, 32 note
γραφαὶ 19
γράφειν, γράφεσθαι, 19
γυιῶσαι, ἀπογυιῶσαι, 12

Δ.

δαίμονα δοῦναι 30
δαίμων, Homeric sense of, 31
δέγμενος, δέχμενος, 28
δεδοκημένος 28
δελτοῦσθαι 19
δέχνυσθαι 29 note

E.

ἐδανὸς 32
ἐδέγμην 29
ἐεργμένος 30. 32
ἐῆος, ἑῆος, ἑοῖο, 7. 24
εἰδῇ, Ϝίδῃ, 28
εἶδος without F, 26
εἴλω, ϜέλϜω, volvo, 27. 32
εἴρερος 22 note
εἴσατο, ἐϜείσατο, 23. 28. 32
ἐκέκαστο 21
ἐλέγμην 29
ἑλίσσειν, ἐλελίξαι, 27—8
ἔλπομαι, Ϝέλπομαι, 26. 28
ἔλσας, ἐλάσας, 27. 32
ἔοιγμεν 29 note
ἑὸς, suus, 24
ἐπιδώμεθα 28 note
ἐπίπιθμεν 29 note
ἐπώχατο 29 note
ἔργον without F, 26
ἐρύω, Ϝερύω, ἐρύσασθαι, 25
ἔρχατο 29 note
ἔσσο, Ϝεσ, 26
εὐαγγέλιον 9
εὔληρα 22 note
ἑὸς 7. 24
εὖτε, ἠύτε, 7

Z.

ζωγρεῖν 32
ζωρότερον πιεῖν 12 note

H.

ἡδὺς without F, 27
ἤμονες ἄνδρες 13
ἦορος, ἄωρος, 32
ἤπειρος, ἄπειρος, 25
ἠσχυμμένος 30
ἠύτε 7

Θ.

Θρῆσσαι σανίδες 18
Θρινακίη, *Trinacria*, 25

I.

ἰδεῖν, Ϝιδεῖν, 25, 26 note, 27
ἰδέω χάριν 28
ἰδυίῃ 28
ἰέναι, ἱέναι, *jacio*, 23 note
Ἴλιον, Ϝίλιον, 25
Ἴρις 26
ἰσχανᾶν 32
Ἶφι, Ϝῖφι, 25

K.

κάζω 21
καίνυμαι 21
καπύσσειν 30
κὰρ, κάρος, Κᾶρος, 25
καταείσατο 23 note
κεκασμένος 21
κελαδεννὰ ἔπη 9
κοῦροι, κουρῆτες, *Curiatii*, 22 note
κοῦρος, *infans*, 22 note
κρήγυον 13

Λ.

λόγιοι 17
λόγοι 17
λογοποιοὶ 17
λῦτο 25
λῶρος, *lorum*, 22 note

M.

μεμορυχμένος 30
μετήορος, μετέωρος, 32
μήδεα φωτὸς 22 note
μνήμη 17

N.

νέποδες, *nepotes*, 13. 22 note

Ξ.

ξεστὸς λίθος 20
ξυνωρὶς 31

O.

ὄαρ, ὄαροι, ὀαρίζειν, 31—2
οἱ for Ϝοι, 26
οἶκος, οἰκία, Ϝ, 26
οἶνος, Ϝοῖνος, 26—7. 31
ὄνασθαι, ὀνόσασθαι, ὀναίμην, ὄνομαι, 23—4
ὁπλότερος 22

ὅρμενος 29
ὅσσεσθαι, Ϝόσσα, 23. 32
ὄχ' ἄριστος 12
ὀψείοντες 21 note

Π.

πάλλεσθαι, ἅλλεσθαι, 32
παρήορος 31
πίνακες 18
πινύσσειν, πινύσκειν, 29—30
πλὴς, πλέες, *plebs*, *locuples*, 22
Ποσίδηιον 25
προθέουσιν 29
προσώπατα 14 note
πρότμησις 14 note

P.

ῥερυπωμένος 30
ῥυσάμην 25

Σ.

σιφλὸς, σιφλῶσαι, 13
σκέπ, σκόπ, 32
σκεπᾶν 30
σκέπτεσθαι 32
στεῦτο, *stabat*, *statuit*, 29
στῆλαι 20
συνάορος 31

T.

ταρπῆναι, τραπῆναι confused, 32
τέμω 30
τετευχὼς, τετευχῆσθαι, 30

Υ.

ὑββάλλειν 12 note
ὑλᾶν 30
ὕλη and *silva*, 28 note
ὑφᾶν 30
uxor 31 note

Φ.

ψίεα 14 note
φέρτερος, φέριστος, 22
φέρτρον, *feretrum*, 22 note
φθῆναί τινος 21 note

X.

χέρηα, χέρης, *herus*, χείρων, χερίων, 22
χήρατο 30

Ω.

ὤνατο 24
ὤρεσσι 31
—ώσσειν, verbs in, 29

Printed by Libri Plureos GmbH in Hamburg,
Germany